Annabella

1

Skipping tune

bouncing

I wish I had a skipp – ing rope.

I'd play with it all morn – ing.

I'd hop and jump and sing the words.

My friends would do the turn – ing.

Flying kites

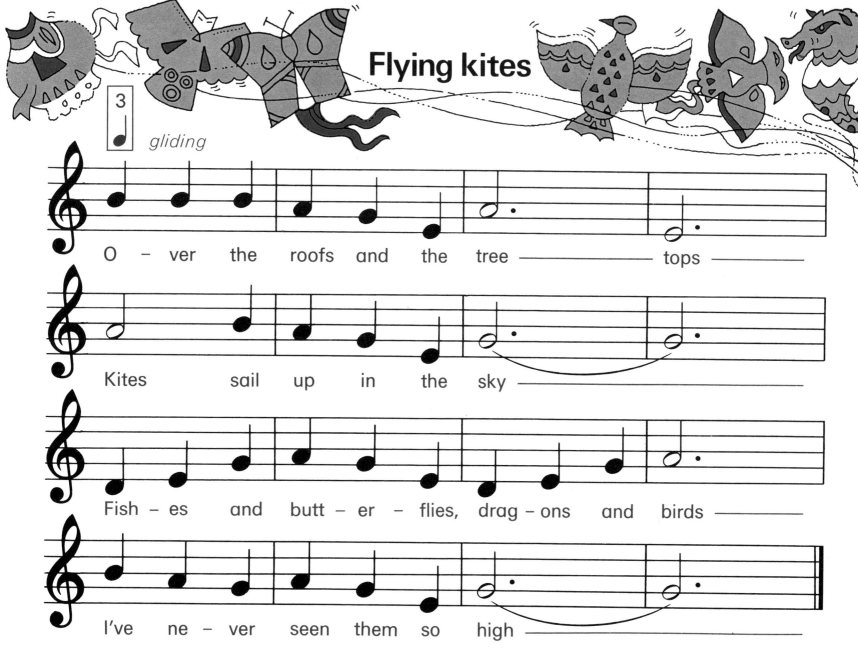

O – ver the roofs and the tree ——— tops ———

Kites sail up in the sky ———

Fish – es and butt – er – flies, drag – ons and birds ———

I've ne – ver seen them so high ———

Donkey cart

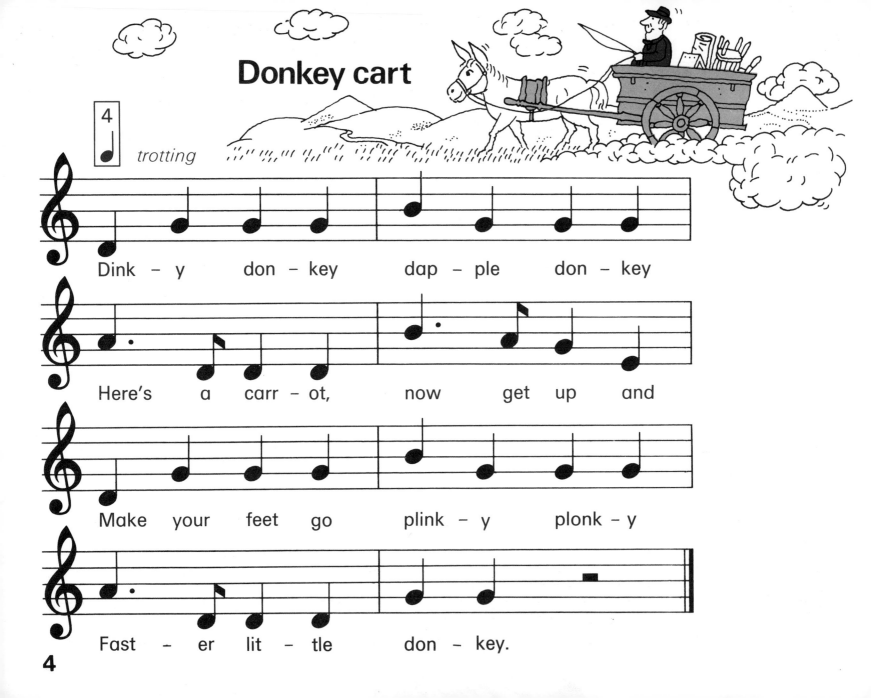

trotting

Dink – y   don – key   dap – ple   don – key

Here's   a   carr – ot,   now   get   up   and

Make   your   feet   go   plink – y   plonk – y

Fast – er   lit – tle   don – key.

4

Pastorale

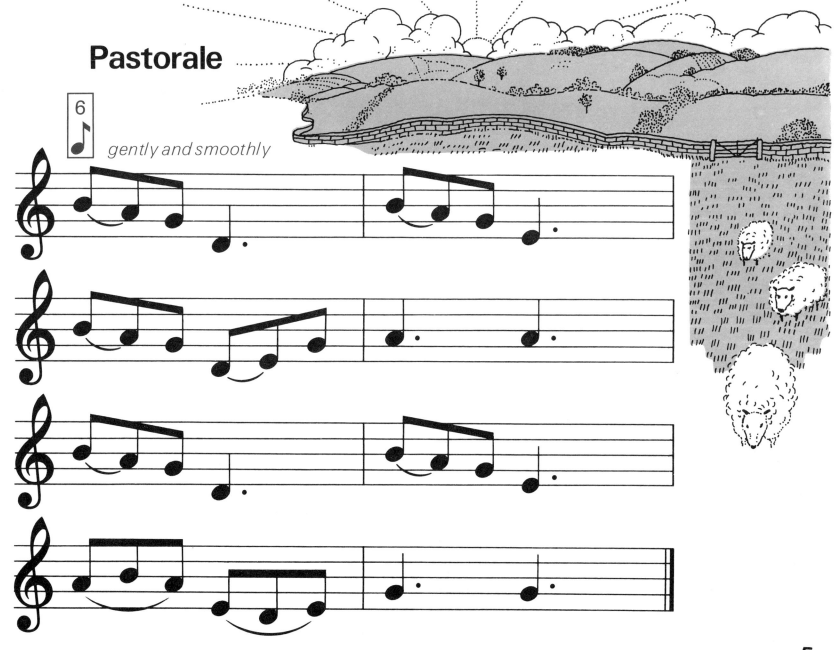

gently and smoothly

Pigs

Round and round the garden

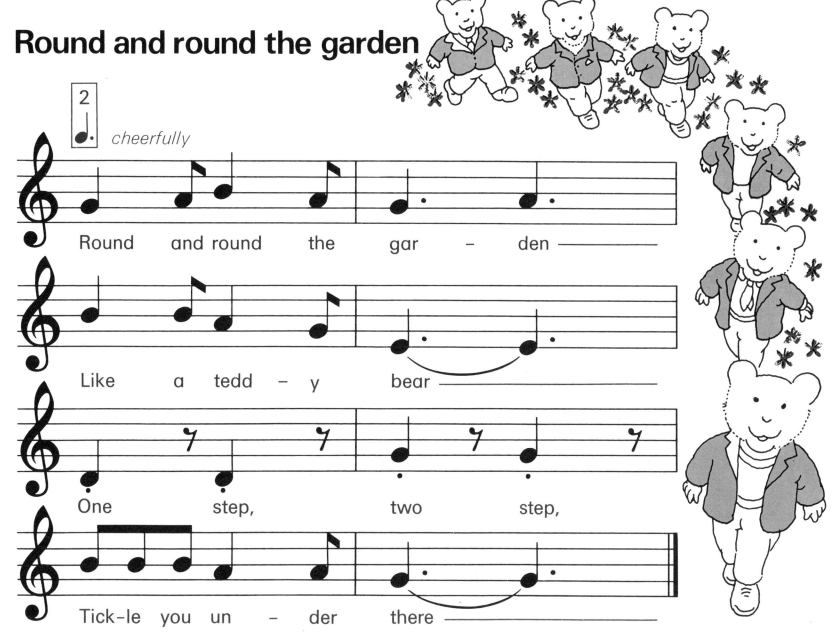

cheerfully

Round and round the gar – den

Like a tedd – y bear

One step, two step,

Tick-le you un – der there

7

Sea shells

Aran

play right through the tune

The End

now play from the beginning to 'The End'

9

Sunshine

Cossack riders

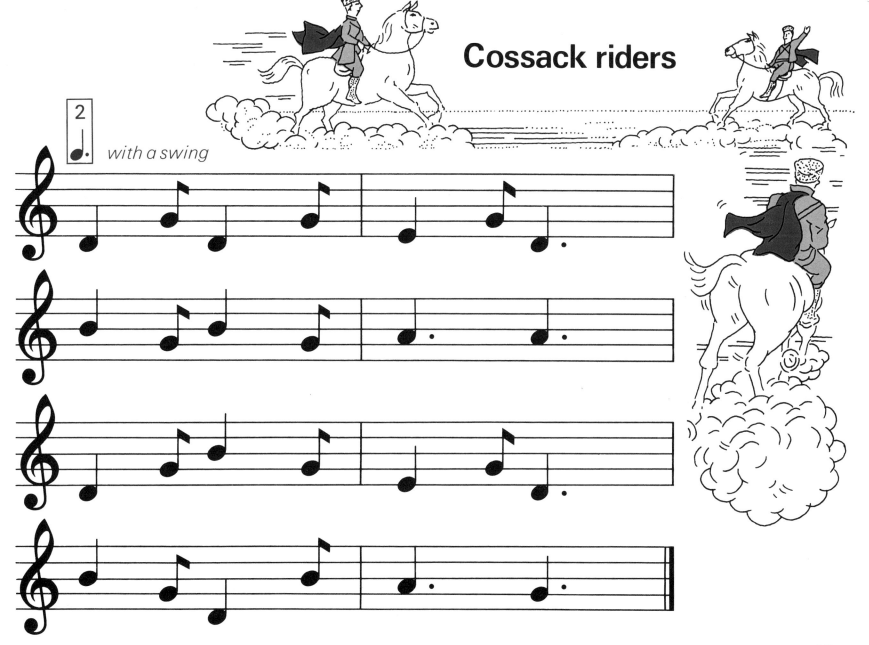

with a swing

Reindeer

left hand at the top

left thumb closed

left thumb open

gently

Sheep are graz - ing on the hill ———

All is peace - ful, all is still ———

The circus is coming

with excitement

D   **C**

Hurr – y   hurr – y   down   the   street.

If   you   don't   you'll   miss   a   treat.

Here   they   come!   Bang   the   drum!

Join   the   long   pro – cess – ion.

Snake charmer

Crofter's song

wistfully

Blue is the mount – ain, blue is the loch and

Blue is the smoke that curls from the croft ——

Blue is the hea – ther, blue is the sky, as

Blue as your eye when you greet —— me ——

Up goes the Big Top

like hammering

Topsy turvy

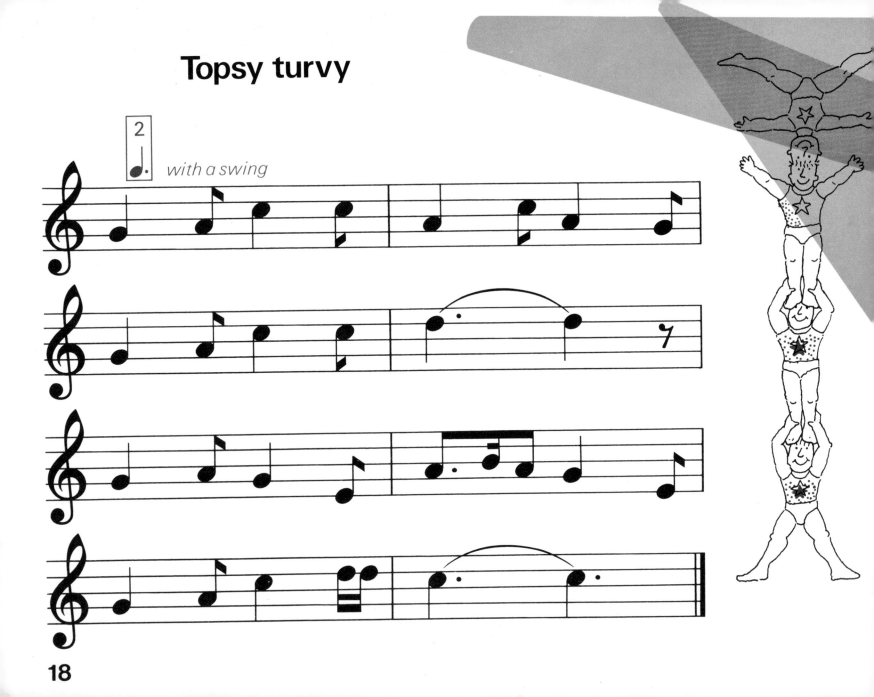

Morris men

cheerfully

Showers

lightly

Rain drops patt - er on the roof and down the wind-ow pane ——— When the sun comes out and shines, we'll all go out a - gain ———

Mountaineers' dance

with energy

getting slower, the second time.

Cowboy

Julius Caesar

4 ♩ *with humour*

Jul – ius Caes – ar, the Rom – an geez – er,

squashed his wife with a lem – on squeez – er !

Whistling Billy

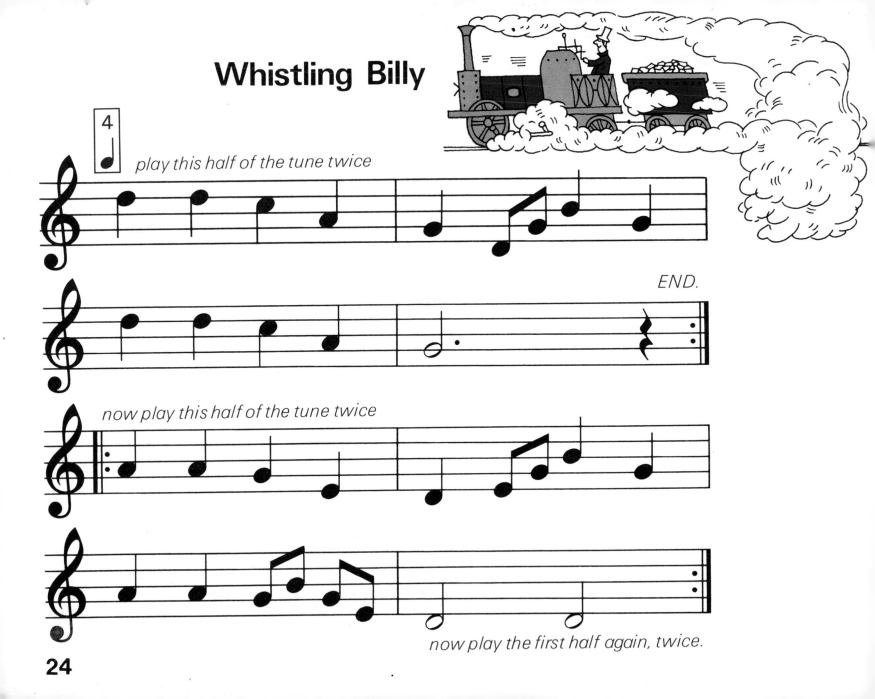

play this half of the tune twice

now play this half of the tune twice

END.

now play the first half again, twice.

24